MILNER CRAFT SERIES

Country Applique

Quick and easy projects

BARBARA NUTT & SUSAN ELLERY

First published in 1997 by
Sally Milner Publishing Pty Ltd
RMB 54 Burra Road
Burra Creek, NSW 2620
Australia

© Barbara Nutt & Susan Ellery, 1997

Design by Amanda Knobel, ANU Graphics, Canberra
Photography by Clive Palmer. Jamestown, SA
Printed in Hong Kong

National Library Cataloguing-in-Publication data:

    Nutt, Barbara.
    Country applique : quick and easy projects.

    ISBN 1 86351 212 8.

    1. Applique. 2. Applique - Patterns. I. Ellery, Susan.
    II. Title. (Series : Milner craft series).

Preface

Orroroo is a small friendly country town, located approximately 350 kms north of Adelaide in South Australia, with a district population of about 950 residents. It is primarily a pastoral and agricultural community, consisting of beef cattle, merino sheep and cropping of wheat, barley, oats and legumes. With an average yearly rainfall of 13 inches or 325 millimetres, it is situated at the foothills of the Flinders Ranges and is an area of great rugged beauty, attracting many tourists.

Susan Ellery and Barbara Nutt have both married into farming families that were part of the original pioneer settlement of the area in the 1870s. While many of the traditions and practices of the settlers have changed, there seems to be a steady 'universal' resurgence of many of the crafts of yesteryear.

Susan and Barbara forged a partnership three years ago, when they came to know each other through friends and a mutual love of craftwork. Sue was an avid quilter and embroiderer, and Barbara was interested in painting and design. While they both loved the look of cross-stitch and patchwork, their modern lifestyles left them much less time to pursue those hobbies. They had both previously worked part-time as Registered Nurses, and they both had to 'pitch-in' on the farm, especially through busy times, like shearing or harvest, whilst meeting the commitments of raising a collective brood of seven kids. They wanted to find a type of craftwork that would give them total country appeal, but without the painstaking hours and hours of dedication needed for traditional crafts. Iron-on applique was the answer — Barbara would create the designs and Sue could sew the finished article.

They quickly produced several hanging pictures for their own homes, from which they received a tremendous response. This led them to start putting together kits, advertising and then selling them through mail order. 'Black Sheep Traders' was born, allowing Barbara and Sue to work from home and to successfully juggle farm, family and community commitments, yet remain creative at the same time.

 # Introduction

Iron-on applique is becoming more and more popular as a modern craft technique, largely because of its simplicity and ease of application. It really is little more than gluing fabrics, using your iron as a tool in doing so.

Iron-on applique can be enjoyed by the absolute beginner, or it can be incorporated with other fabric crafts, patchwork and quilting for example, to create a much more challenging craft project. Your work may also be embellished with embroidery and accessories (buttons and bows) to create a very intricate pattern.

In this book we have concentrated upon home furnishings and clothing, however the applications of iron-on applique are not limited to those mediums. We have successfully transformed the following: heat-proof blinds, wooden plaques, wooden crates, paper and cardboard.

When ironing onto a backing where stitching is not possible, or not desired, a fine tip marking pen or laundry marker is what you need, to mark on eyes or feet, or to give faux stitching lines to a piece of work.

The basic principles to remember when applying iron-on applique and following our designs include:

1. Whichever direction your pattern faces, this will be reversed when you have traced and transferred it onto your fabric base.

2. Applique pieces should be overlapped when in a multi-piece design to help hold the picture together.
   Some care should be taken to ensure that you overlap in the correct order.

3. For the backing fabric we have given a larger size than the finished project, to allow for ease of framing, as all our designs start from the centre and work outwards.

Contents

" don't aim for "perfection", aim for charm "

Before You Begin

It is most important that you read through the instructions carefully before you begin. Then ensure that you have all of your required tools and materials ready.

You will need:

IRON-ON FUSIBLE WEBBING: double sided glue with tracing paper on one side.

FABRICS: of your choice. We would recommend 100% cottons. We use mainly small repetitive spots, checks, plains & mini florals.

BACKING FABRIC OR BASE PROJECT: measurements for fabric are given on project page, and allow for framing.

SHARP SCISSORS: smaller scissors are handy for smaller projects.

LEAD PENCIL: for tracing, also eraser & ruler are handy.

IRON: and ironing board.

EMBROIDERY NEEDLE & THREADS: we have used in this book DMC green: 890, wheat: 422, black: 310, burgundy: 814.

LAUNDRY MARKER: optional

To give an aged look to your fabric, we have used the following recipe:

Thoroughly wet your base fabric, or whatever you wish to antique. Wring out and soak in a bowl of strong tea + 1 teaspoon of coffee mix. Remove when happy with depth of colour; dry, iron & begin!

This is suitable for pictures only, as it will eventually get lighter with frequent washing on a garment.

Instructions

1. Press all fabrics using iron on moderate setting with steam. Find centre of your base fabric or project and mark with a pin, or fold and iron. This will give you a starting point.

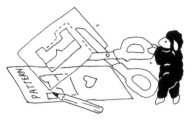

2. Place applique film over pattern page and trace your shapes onto paper side with a sharp pencil. Roughly cut around shape leaving a small border.

3. Place paper piece rough (glue side) down, onto the BACK of your coloured fabric and iron-on until fused. DO NOT use steam. Set iron to medium hot for cotton fabrics. We recommend you do a test iron first.

4. Now cut around pencil lines neatly, peel backing from fabric and arrange onto base fabric — as shown in photo. Use your central marker as a guide.

5. Use your ruler to check distances and get an even finish. For detailed projects that require quite a bit of layering, use a pin to ease pieces into place. You may also lightly 'touch' iron to hold the project in place. When you are happy with placement, iron-on well. You might find that you may be required to stabilise your picture again by ironing, as you stitch other areas at a later date.

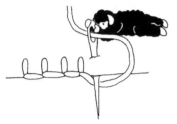

Blanket Stitch

6. Blanket stitch around shapes with embroidery needle and 2 strands of DMC threads. This serves to hold pieces in place and also is decorative, especially if done in a contrasting thread colour

Running Stitch

7. Running stitch gives a shadow effect around your design. Its use is optional. We choose to use 3 strands for this lovely shadow effect. It is also a quilting stitch, sandwiching the three layers securely together.

Back Stitch

8. For that finishing touch on some projects a phrase or some form of lettering may be added. To do this, practise your letters on paper and, when you have the right size and spacing, trace them onto your fabric or project. You may use a light box, or tape fabric against a window and trace by sunlight. Very lightly trace on words with a lead pencil then either mark them on with a laundry marker, or stitch them 'Back stitch'

14

with 2 or 3 strands of DMC. Don't be afraid to use your own handwriting, even the most awful script will look good when you add a little black dot at the points.

9. When you have completed your project, give it a final iron. If you have included quite a bit of stitching, give a light steam iron on the back of your project to help bring up stitches evenly. Using a soft fluffy towel when ironing has its benefits also.

Fresh Milk

You will need the requirements listed on page 11, but as well you will need the following extras:

> Backing fabric, 62 cm wide x 53 cm high
> (24" wide x 21")
> Black thread colour
> Wheat thread colour
> Border—5 cm (2") wide strips
> Corner squares—8 cm (3") squares

'Daisy', our one and only milking cow, is the inspiration for all of our cow designs. She's never actually been milked but was purchased to foster orphaned calves from the commercial beef cattle herd. Today she lives a life of semi-retirement and only looks after calves of her own.

Bruce Walter, a friend of Sue's, framed this design for us using recycled Baltic floor boards and then cleverly mounted a strip of rusty old barbed wire around it, which gives a very rustic finish. However, if you don't have such clever friends or don't want to frame professionally, buy your frame, first distress it if need be, and then make your picture to fit the frame. You can easily add or chop off a bit of background, or alternately, patterns are easy to enlarge or reduce on a photocopier.

To achieve an aged look, we often use the reverse side of a print fabric. The backing fabric here was a blue check.

Starting with your arrow, trace and cut out the pattern in one piece (remember to allow for reversal), then copy or trace on lettering. Layer arrow over cow's feet, udder under body and then put patches on. Don't iron until you're happy. Use your ruler to measure equal distances to position borders.

There is another version of 'Fresh Milk' on the 'House & Hearts' page 24. Note that you would need to leave more space at the bottom of your arrow to overlap hearts and buttons in that version.

When you have finished ironing, blanket stitch and then add running stitch for the tail and the verse. Add shadow stitching in 3 strands of black DMC to finish off.

Pattern—Fresh Milk

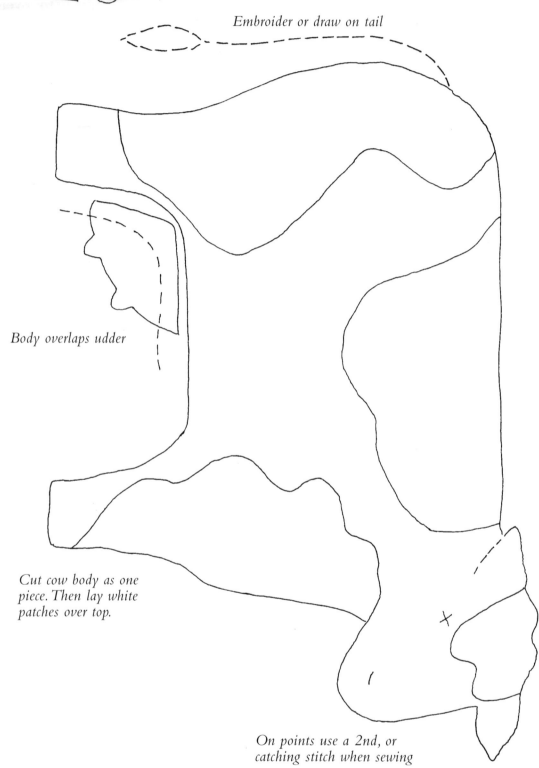

Embroider or draw on tail

Body overlaps udder

Cut cow body as one piece. Then lay white patches over top.

On points use a 2nd, or catching stitch when sewing

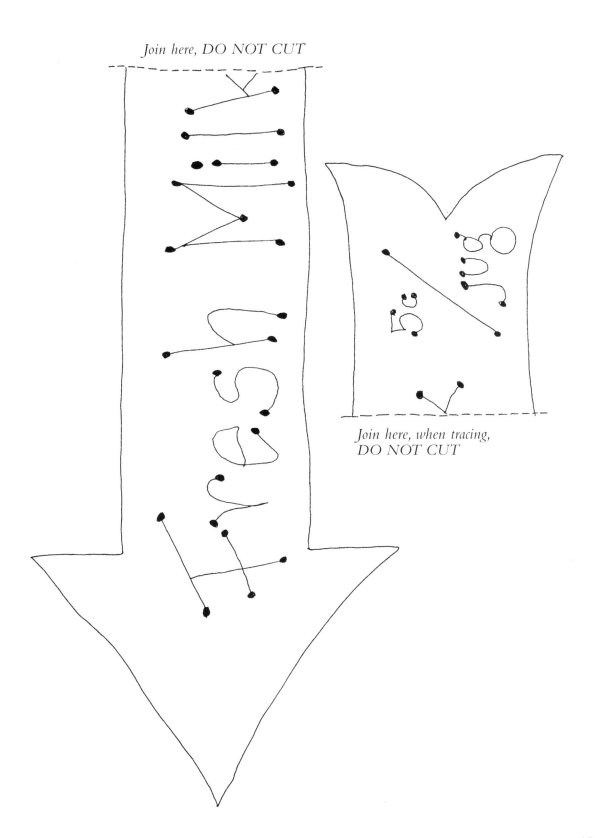

Join here, DO NOT CUT

Join here, when tracing,
DO NOT CUT

19

Country Kitchen

You will need the requirements listed on page 11, but as well you will need the following extras:

> Oven mits, teatowels, etc
> DMC thread as listed on page 11

These pigs and apples give a simple country flavour to any kitchen accessory and are easily completed in less than an hour. They look terrific on an apron or even on a kitchen blind or curtains.

Decorating a teatowel or oven mit is a really inexpensive way of creating a handmade gift for a friend or relative who is especially hard to buy for. The little rooster has been ironed straight onto a recycled brown paper notepad. Follow exactly the same instructions but ensure that you don't have the steam on your iron when ironing paper products or they will curl up.

Your can create you own gift wrap and greeting cards with any of the smaller designs. They are very easy to do and unique!

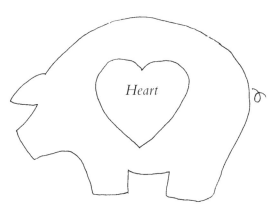

Heart

Draw or embroider
stem & seed

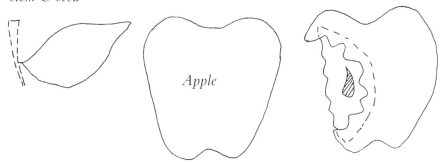

Apple

Head

Wing

Neck

Body

Roof

Mark on nails

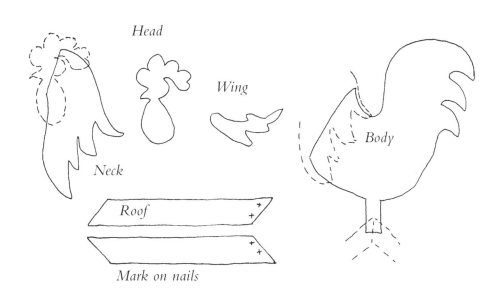

House & Hearts

You will need the requirements listed on page 11, but as well you will need the following extras:

> Backing fabric, 35 cm wide x 30 cm high
> (13" x 11")
> Buttons
> Cushion cover

This framed house and hearts design looks great in a mix of colours — red or green for example, or in shades of one colour. Then finish off with a family or house name. This is a lovely gift for a family leaving a town or suburb.

The hearts are so easy to sew on garments as well — to dress up a T shirt, or patch over knee holes in a little girl's jeans. The clothes in our photo have been recycled from older brother's shirt and vest, much to his horror!

The small framed cow can be completed very quickly but looks very intricate when finished with flowers embroidered around its neck using French or colonial knots.

The 'Fresh Milk' design has here been transferred onto a pre-made cushion, in different colour ways and then dressed up with buttons and hearts and given a plaited tail. It took only 2 hours to complete.

French or Colonial Knots

*1. Bring thread up through
fabric, wrap around needle*

*2. Pull needle through and
you are left with a knot*

Pattern—House & Hearts

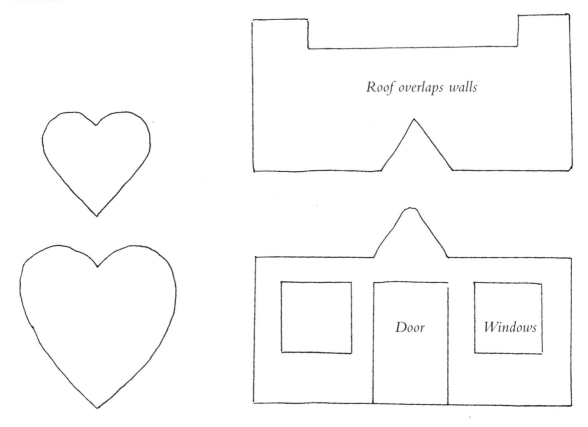

Roof overlaps walls

Door *Windows*

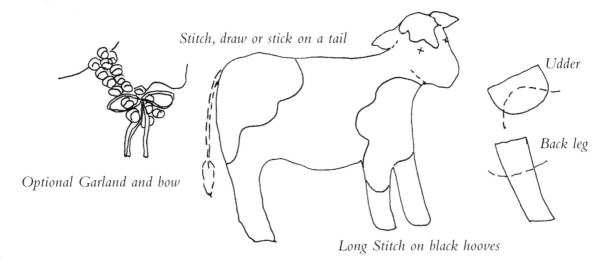

Fringe may be embroidered on

Stitch, draw or stick on a tail

Udder

Back leg

Optional Garland and bow

Long Stitch on black hooves

Fresh Milk

Country Kitchen

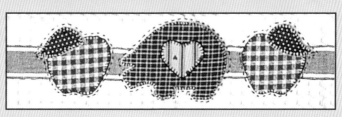

House & Hearts

Bacon & Eggs

Blue Friendship Wreath

Laundry Day

Laundry Day

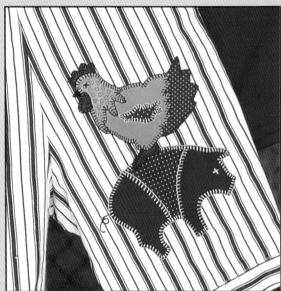

Bacon & Eggs

You will need the requirements listed on page 11, but as well you will need the following extras:

> Backing fabric, seeded calico 50 cm wide x 56 cm high (20" x 22")

Chickens are a favourite feature in the decoration of our kitchens, and it's great to have your own hens and egg supply on the farm, but they can make your blood boil when you catch them in your garden!

For this picture, the frame was salvaged from an old screen door, made from red pine (once again by Bruce Walter) and the checked fabric surround is an effective alternative to expensive mounting. To make the keyhole shape we traced 3/4 of the way around a large dinner plate and then measured a rectangle (31.5cm wide x 14cm high, 12 1/2" x 5 1/2"), allowing 33 cm (13") from the top of the plate to the bottom of the rectangle.

When using a checked fabric such as we did, you can iron-on the fabric in several pieces, but if you choose a plain surround, you will need to iron it on in one large piece. First centre your arrow and post, then layer the hearts on.

Position your animals and arrow and iron when you are happy with their placement, taking care to tuck the feet under correctly.

The tail and lettering can be either marked on with pen or stitched using back stitch. We also stitched over the chicken's beak using 3 strands of black thread.

 # Pattern—Bacon & Eggs

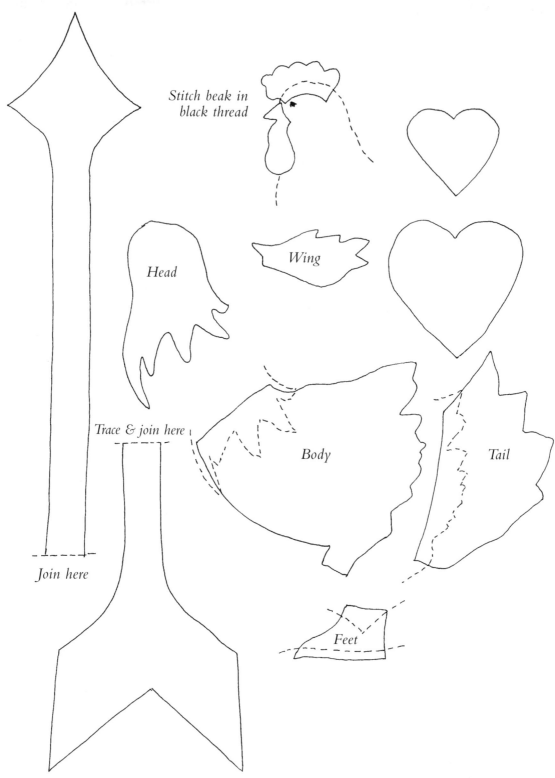

Stitch beak in black thread

Head

Wing

Body

Tail

Trace & join here

Join here

Feet

34

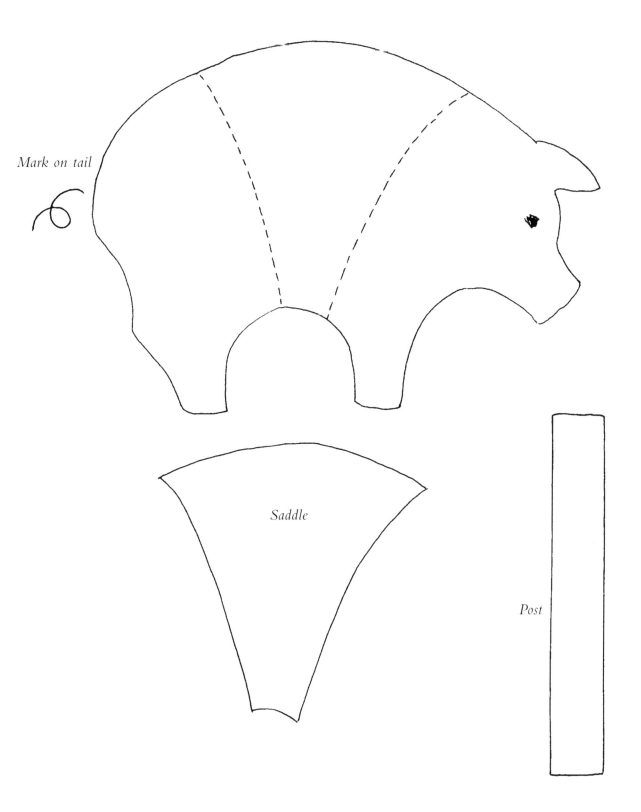

Mark on tail

Saddle

Post

Blue Friendship Wreath

You will need the requirements listed on page 11, but as well you will need the following extras:

> Backing fabric, 50 cm x 50 cm (20"x 20")
> Checked fabric
> Assorted blue scraps in navy toning

This design was created as a gift for a special friend, and when a personal message is included, it certainly is a gift that will be treasured forever.

It is a very simple pattern and very easy to assemble with only 4 basic shapes in the design.

The same arrangement looks great in pastel pinks and blues on cushions in bedrooms and also in Federation reds and greens.

If you cheat a bit and buy ready made cushion covers and then applique on to them you'll have a finished product in no time at all.

To get your circular shape, use a dinner plate and lightly mark on with a lead pencil onto your backing fabric. A ruler will help you gain accurate symmetrical placement of flowers and leaves.

Leaf cut 8

Daisy cut 3

Tulip cut 6

Cut 1

Large heart cut 1

Medium heart cut 3

Cut 6

Circle optional

Laundry Day

You will need the requirements listed on page 11, but as well you will need the following extras:

    Clothing on which to apply fabric
    Scraps of different types of fabric

Keeping up with the latest trends in kids clothing is never easy, but with a few scraps of material and a little imagination, you can transform an ordinary item into a much loved favourite.

The sheep and windmill are quickly applied to a little boy's pillow case and also look great on pyjamas.

Andrew's train looks fabulous on fabric and then hung in a frame for his bedroom.

The chicken and pig have been transferred from Bacon & Eggs onto the overalls with directions reversed, and look just as good when placed singularly onto a T shirt, or up the leg of jeans.

Why not take the baby pig and chicken and use them as patches over stains or holes. Kids will love them and no-one will know!

Even a simple square patch can look very trendy when you use co-ordinating fabrics and threads.

Our children regularly get lovely compliments about their clothing, and often we are covering a hole made climbing through the barbed wire fences on our farms.

Pattern—Laundry Day

Windmill legs cut 4

Windmill fans—cut 8

Top of windmill tower

Carriage cut as many as needed

Pattern —Laundry Day continued

Baby chicken

Dotted line may be stitched or drawn on

Baby pig

Angels

Gifts & Cards

Home Sweet Home

The Daisy Chain

Our Story Quilt

Daisy from Wreath

Angels

You will need the requirements listed on page 11, but as well you will need the following extras:

> Backing: woollen blanket 60 cm x 80 cm
> (24" x 32")
> Paper, cards
> Windcheaters

Little girls just love angels and fairies and they'll love these two. One flying and one standing, they look terrific in pinks and blues, and also in Christmas colours on plain wrapping paper or cards.

If you have young children, you'll know how much they love to hear about the 'tooth-fairy' and we've created a tiny wall-hanging with a thimble for a bucket and a little golden wand.

For a more naive-looking fairy elongate the arms and legs and use deeper colours.

The angel flying on the windcheater includes two wooden buttons and is a favourite to wear.

The baby's woollen rug is just the right size to fit into a baby's capsule or to overlay in the pram.

Wool is a divine medium, but a little care needs to be taken when ironing on your design. Put it into place and then carefully cover with a teatowel and lightly iron. Then check all is in place correctly and complete ironing on the fairies. Instead of using buttons for decorations, we tied up some tiny double coloured bows for a slight change.

We modified the pattern of the 'Tooth Fairy', by not tracing the wing pattern, to make a little girl which we have used for one of our quilt blocks.

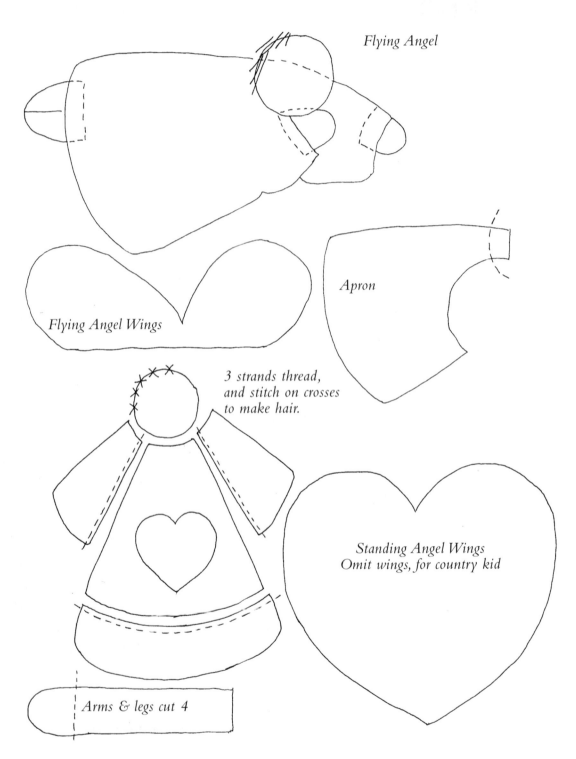

Flying Angel

Flying Angel Wings

Apron

3 strands thread,
and stitch on crosses
to make hair.

*Standing Angel Wings
Omit wings, for country kid*

Arms & legs cut 4

Gifts & Cards

You will need the requirements listed on page 11, but as well you will need the following extras:

Good quality card or paper
Inexpensive garments

These small designs are very quick to complete and can be applied to most surfaces that can take heat. If you have trouble with tiny pieces adhering, eg. wheels on the train, stick them down with glue.

Nothing beats a handmade card for that special occasion, but for little more expense you can make a lasting gift when you make them up and then place them into an inexpensive frame. Remove the glass and dress them up with tiny extras like buttons for wheels, or make a tiny wand out of a matchstick and gold star.

The cow has a bow made from DMC thread and small embroidered flowers around its neck, and grass has been added to the foreground using long stitch. It is framed in recycled Baltic pine floorboards again. Note that if you are using any three-dimensional items such as buttons, then small spaces need to be put behind the glass to allow for the added thickness.

 # *Pattern—Gifts & Cards*

*Cut as many wheels as you need,
buttons are easier*

*Optional bow and rose buds
(French knots) make garland*

*See House & Hearts
for French knot
instructions*

Udder

Back leg

Long Stitch (3 strands) for hooves

Home Sweet Home

You will need the requirements listed on page 11, but as well you will need the following extras:

> Backing fabric: 55 cm wide x 50 cm high or (21" x 19")

House and garden use various scraps, small repeating florals and tiny checks amongst plain fabrics, giving plenty of scope for variety in your garden.

This lovely little cottage was based around Barbara's first home. It was a typical stone cottage in a country town, two main rooms, a hallway and the rest had been tacked onto the back.

We injected lots of blood, sweat and tears and the little cottage soon became a home. Unfortunately, the garden never quite realised its potential, as it has in this design, brimming with hollyhocks and daisies, a rose arbour and hedge-covered picket fence.

This project has plenty of scope for embroidery if you so desire, although the use of floral fabrics gives a very effective finish.

Quite a lot of layering is involved with the assembly of this project and it is important to follow the layering guide. X marks the centre of the project. Remember, don't iron until you are happy with the layout.

The Home Sweet Home motto is easily traced through onto fabric, then back stitched over with your choice of thread colour. The thinnest of guttering on the roof was glued and not stitched.

The house looks striking on a cushion, and you may choose to add you own garden plan to the front of this house for an even more personal approach.

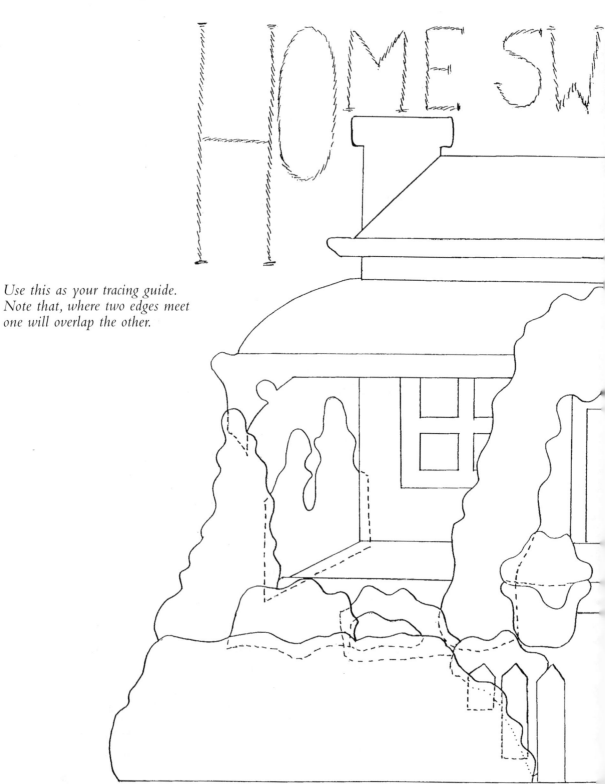

Use this as your tracing guide.
Note that, where two edges meet
one will overlap the other.

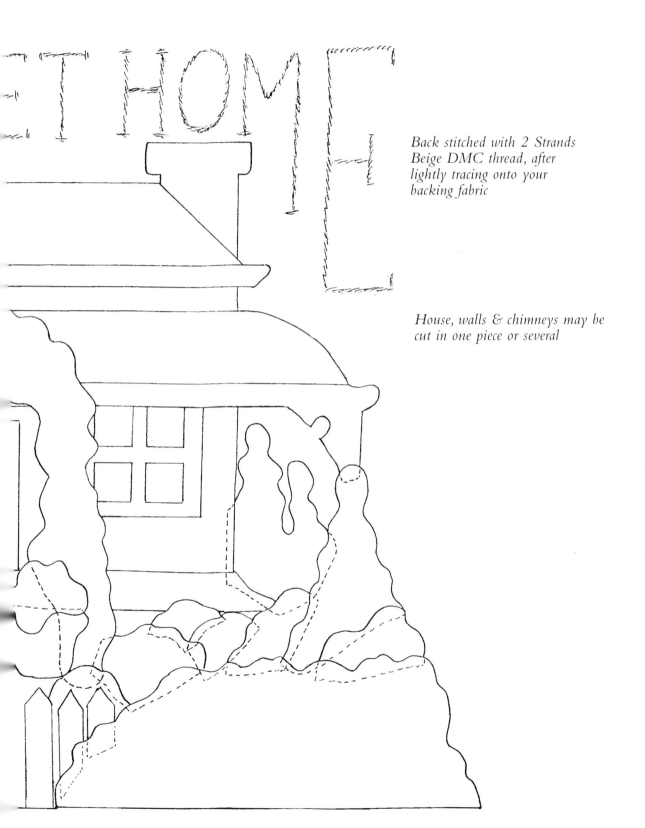

Back stitched with 2 Strands
Beige DMC thread, after
lightly tracing onto your
backing fabric

House, walls & chimneys may be
cut in one piece or several

The Daisy Chain

You will need the requirements listed on page 11, but as well you will need the following extras:

> Daisy and/or sunflower fabric
> Suitable clothing

There are so many wonderful fabrics available, sometimes they are hard to resist. We couldn't leave this sunflower and daisy check behind, it was just perfect for a special party dress. The daisy swag on the yoke was the finishing touch. It was inspired by a sister-in-law's beautiful smocked dresses, but with iron-on applique. The work was done in only a couple of hours and ready for a party the next day.

You can apply the same principle to any favourite fabric, simply pick out some elements, enlarge the design and as long as the shapes are reasonably simple, you can iron and applique them onto any matching accessories.

 # Pattern—Daisy Chain

← —— *Use the same layout on the other side*

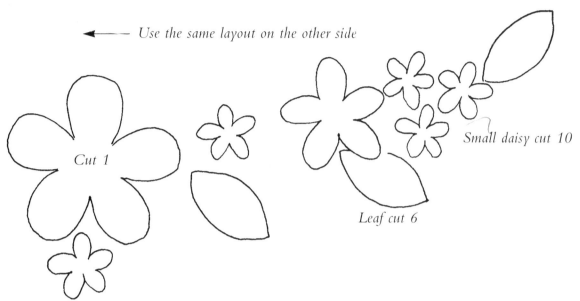

Cut 1

Small daisy cut 10

Leaf cut 6

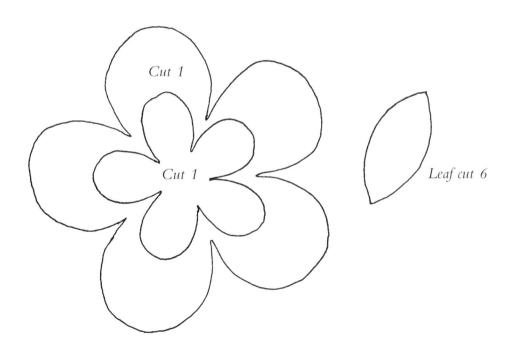

Cut 1

Cut 1

Leaf cut 6

Our Story Quilt

This project started with a wreath that Barbara designed for Susan. We have a great love of garland floral wreath designs and use them both as flower decorations in our homes, as well as appliqued and embroidered designs onto quilts and pictures.

For a different look we decided at the very last moment to turn the Centre Feature Block into a quilt, rather than a framed picture. The quilt uses few patterns and a maximum of 20 fabrics throughout, but use as many as you feel suits your own home.

We appliqued the Centre Features Block onto seeded or dress calico and the surrounding designs have been taken from other projects throughout this book: hearts, plus house and hearts from pattern number 3, little girl from pattern number 7, (angel less wings plus longer legs), plus the Forget-me-nots bouquet from pattern number 5.

The wreath uses bits and pieces from throughout the book and therefore is a good way of combining our designs in different ways.

Making the Wreath
(or central part of quilt)

You'll need a big bag of fabric scraps to make this wonderful country wreath. We used a total of 20 different materials, and some were used in reverse to give yet another variation (the roses for example).

Don't forget to antique any fabrics for a more aged look (see page 12).

Trace and cut out your shapes. Of course you don't necessarily have to use as many pieces as we have — a less ornate wreath can work just as well. And in the centre of the wreath, there is room for a verse if you prefer.

You will need (we used):

> Calico — cut 20"(50 cm) square
> DMC threads — green 890 , wheat 422,
> black 310, burgundy 814
> Sharp scissors
> HB pencil, rubber and ruler
> bag of scrap cotton fabrics
> large dinner plate (to trace a circle with)
> camera or a door 'peep hole' - this allows you to check colour placements, by looking through it at your applique work or fabric choices

NOTE: Always sew on straight grain, so your picture does not pucker.

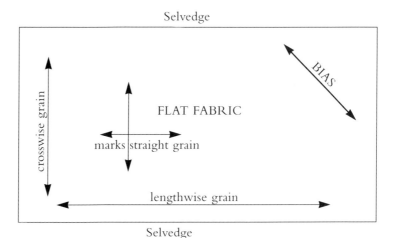

Figure 1

To obtain your rounded shape, lightly trace around a dinner plate, which has been placed a little above centre point to allow for the depth of the rose garland or wreath.

From here you will build up the lower sides and base to give the teardrop shape.

Place your bow slightly off centre. The ribbon sections can go on anytime, depending on whether you would like them to be a major or minor feature.

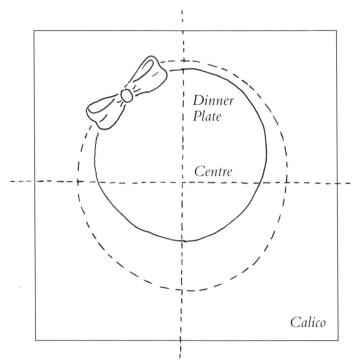

Figure 2

Start building up your wreath by placing the larger shapes on first and gradually adding smaller pieces, over-lapping them as you go, as you can see in the photograph. You may need to move your various coloured flowers and leaves around until you achieve the right balance.

You may wish to substitute coloured buttons for the small centres of flowers and cut down your sewing time, but apply them at the very end of this project.

When you are happy with how your wreath looks, iron and stitch into place.

Press well and then you are ready to frame. Or you may wish to make this central design into a quilt, as we have done.

Leaf 1–cut 4

Leaf 2–cut 13

Leaf 3–cut 16

x 19

Cut 6

Cut 3

Cut 3

Cut 3

Bud
x 2

x 2

Rose cut 2

Cut 2

Cut 2

To make rose bud fold
in as shown

French knots
and straight
stitch used on
this lily

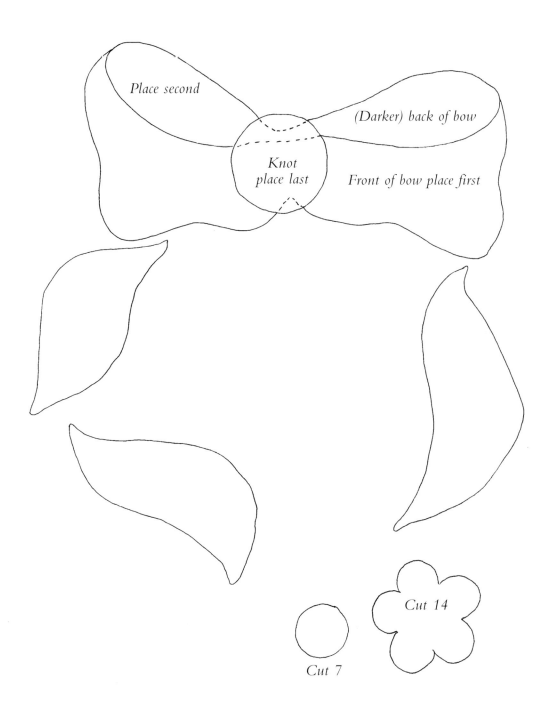

Place second

(Darker) back of bow

Knot
place last

Front of bow place first

Cut 14

Cut 7

Making up the Story Quilt

You will need:

Quilting stencils or patterns
Thread—'Quilter's thread'
Beeswax–optional–to drag your thread through to make it stronger and to prevent it knotting
HB Pencil
Clean white rubber (to erase any excess lines)
Ruler, pins
Quilter's needles—'Betweens' number 10–12
Thimble—optional
Batting or wadding
Backing fabric
Sewing machine and matching good thread

NOTE: Finished size as shown in photograph is 58"(147 cms) square

BATTING OR WADDING: This is the filling which gives a quilt its lovely texture and warmth. We prefer to use the wool and nylon mix, which is a little more expensive, but far softer to work with, and is also a by-product of our district, as it uses wool from the Merino sheep. So what could be more perfect?

Allow movement in any batting you buy by letting it 'loose', so its weave can ease a little, before cutting your required amount.

QUILTER'S THREAD: The thread colour you choose depends on the finished effect you require. We used a medium beige on cream calico, as we wanted the stitches to show, and be part of the overall decoration. But by using an even darker coloured thread, you can get a very stunning effect, providing your stitches are very neat and even. Probably the safest combination is a thread colour to match your backing fabric, if you are just learning.

Quilting the Wreath

The wreath was totally quilted and finished before the outer pictures were added on, as it's easier to quilt smaller items and then join them.

You will need:

> Wadding or batting cut 26"(66 cm) square
> Backing fabric cut 27"(69 cm) square

A. The grid design.

The wreath was quilted in a grid design. This is simple yet stunning.

Using an HB pencil and a narrow but long ruler, carefully draw from corner to corner, using the narrow ruler to set the distances between each line. It pays to spend time setting this up prior to drawing the lines on. Then cross draw, to get the diagonal checkerboard effect, using as many lines as you like. Don't forget to rule the gaps between each little leaf or flower.

Then rule a line all the way around the outer edge at the diameter measurement of 18 1/2"(47 cm) square as this will become the line for machine sewing the first fabric border on.

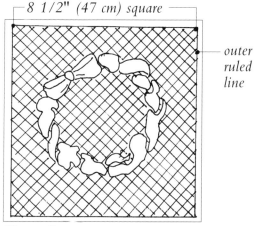

Figure 3

B. Tacking

Once you have drawn your design on to your appliqued block, it's time now to put all the layers together by sandwiching the wool/nylon wadding between the top and base fabric.

First, smooth out any wrinkles and start to pin it in place ready for tacking.

Knot the end of your thread. Starting in the centre, and using a large tacking stitch, fan out the rows from the centre. The bigger the picture to quilt the more tacking is advised, as this stabilises the three layers.

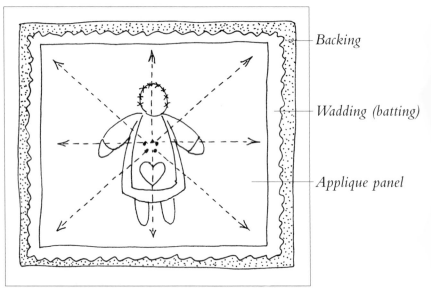

Figure 4. Tacking into place

C. Quilting

Thread your quilting needle ('Between') with quilting thread (and wax it—optional). Tie a small knot at the end. This needs to be pulled up from the base and then needs to lodge in the wadding as an anchor.

Figure 5. Anchoring your quilting thread

Using small running stitches, follow the grid design you have drawn on your applique piece. Start in the centre of your design, and quilt to the outer edges, finishing with a small knot that you pull and weave again through the wadding. If using a false back method (see below) then the knots on the back to start and finish will be hidden.

The quilting should extend to the external pencil line.

Figure 6. Quilting or running stitches

Complete all the necessary quilting. (*Do not* iron as any creases will ease themselves out.) Carefully remove all the tacking stitches.

Your central wreath is now ready to sew to its fabric frames.

Fabric frames around wreath

You will need:

> First frame: cut fabric 2 1/2"(7cm) wide x
> 94"(238 cm) long
> Second frame: cut fabric 1 1/4"(3 cm) wide x
> 102"(258 cm) long

Divide the lengths into 4 equal pieces and machine sew into place, catching just the top layers (and not the wadding or backing which were larger than the wreath panel and should therefore be large enough to provide backing for the frames as well once they are added).

This machine sewing will come right up to the edge of your quilting and look wonderful. Mitre corners if you desire.

Once framed, the wreath with 2 colour borders will measure 24 sq inches (or 61 cm) plus seam allowances.

 # Extending the quilt

As I needed to extend this quilt to fit a Queen size bed, I just kept adding borders until I reached the desired size.

But I have had requests to make the quilt just to the first check border, so these measurements are given here.

I actually made up 12 small panels, as photographed, but by cutting panels in large sections, you can cut down on the work load and machine sewing.

You will need:

> Cut 2 pieces of calico: 25" (65 cm) x 14" (34.5 cm) for A & B (includes seam allowance of 1/4")
> Cut 2 pieces of calico: 51 1/2" (130 cm) x 14" (34.5 cm) for C & D (includes seam allowance of 1/4")

(See figure 7)

Divide these panels into design areas, and check that your designs look just right against your wreath. Use the peep hole lens or your camera to view your colour balance. It's just amazing what difference this little aid makes.

Cut out, iron on, and applique any pictures you wish to add into place using a DMC thread in a contrast colour to that of your fabric, for a wonderful effect. If in doubt, black thread looks fabulous on all fabrics.

Steam iron well your finished picture strips, leaving any buttons until last, as they only catch up the quilting thread.

Then, trace on your quilting pattern, remembering that simple is often the most stunning.

Quilting the extra panels

You will need:

> Cut 2 pieces of wadding/batting: 28" (71 cm) x 16" (41 cm) — for A & B
> Cut 2 pieces of wadding/batting: 56" (142 cm) x 16" (41 cm) — for C & D
> Cut 4 pieces backing fabric allowing extra 5 cm (2") all around on measurements above

(See Figure 7)

Tack and set up your panels as described in Tacking and later in Quilting (page 66).

When finished, remove the tacking thread and lightly rub out any pencil lines showing. Sew on any buttons or decorations.

Piecing the quilt

Attach your panels in the order shown here, making sure you pin them all carefully and view your work objectively before you start machine sewing. Remember, it's only the top layer that is sewn at this stage. So pin your wadding and backing fabric back out of the way.

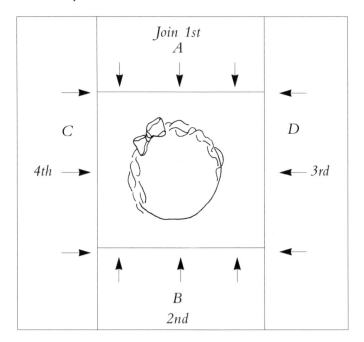

Figure 7

 # Adding last borders

You will need:

> Cut in contrast fabric, joining to make 1 3/4" (4.5 cm) x 212" (540 cm)

Sew this border into place, mitring corners if you like.

Optional — add the next calico border, joining to make the length. Cut in calico, 2 3/4" (7 cm) wide x 232" (592 cm).

Mitre corners if you like.

Cut wadding and backing to suitable size for these extra panels.

HINT: If you have chosen to add extra width, remember to keep in mind, once setting up your three layers, that the outside edge of each panel needs to have the extra wadding and calico backing showing, as this will then have the tops added to it as you go.

Once you have reached your required size by adding extra panels, the top of the quilt is complete.

 # Tidying up the back

Turn your quilt over, face down on your table or the floor.

Now it's time to carefully join all the wadding seams together. Bring the two opposite edges together and gently trim these, so that once they are sewn they will sit flat. If you are a little short in a spot the wadding is very easy to ease out to make the distance.

Thread up a needle and knot the end of the thread, then do a weaving flat stitch by picking up both sides midway through and this will hold your wadding together.

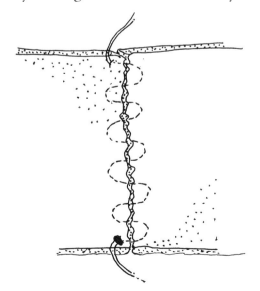

Figure 8. Joining wadding pieces

Once all the wadding has been joined, the end is in sight!

Now, neatly arrange the backing pieces, so they overlap each other and remain flat and tidy. Neatly sew these panels down using a slip or hem stitch, trimming off any excess. If you are using a false back then you can be very quick with this as it won't be showing.

False backs

Trim and tidy up the edges of your quilt. Make sure it measures squarely before you start cutting.

Measure sides plus midway across the quilt, to calculate the exact amount of fabric needed. You will need to join 2 pieces to get the width necessary.

We use a check (or floral) for the backing fabrics. Even though we love using cream fabrics, sometimes they just don't suit our rural dusty environment.

Lay the sewn false backing on the table or floor (face down), then gently smooth out any wrinkles and place on top of your finished quilt, smoothing out once again any little creases. Attach all pieces using the tie method (next page).

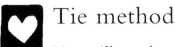 # Tie method

You will need:

> Crochet cotton or Perle cottons
> Heavy duty needle (sharp point)
> Buttons — optional

Using your chosen thread, start towards the centre of your quilt. We tend to use corners and equal distances in a pattern so the tying also forms part of the decoration.

Take your thread through all the layers of the quilt, leaving both tails of the thread on top. Allow quite a bit of length too, as you then tie with double knots, buttons and knots or bows to end off. Each one looks just great.

If you do not like this 'tuffy' look, then start your ties on the back of your quilt, and finish off underneath. Don't pull these ties too tightly, as they may cause a hole.

Figure 9. Tying a Quilt

Binding

Trim the edges of your quilt, if necessary. Attach any buttons or decorations you like at this stage.

Cut the chosen binding on the straight grain, joining to make the required length.

You will need:

> *Binding:* 3 1/2" (9 cm) wide x outside edge measurements of quilt (i.e. sides x 2, top and bottom), plus extra for corners

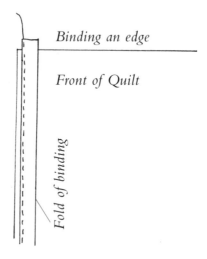

Binding an edge

Front of Quilt

Fold of binding

Figure 10

Fold the strip in half lengthwise and press. With right sides facing, pin and then machine sew the binding.

Mitre or fold under corners.

Turn back binding, pin and hand stitch in place, using strong matching thread.

Finishing

Use a rubber and remove any pencil marks gently.

Don't forget to sign and date the back of your quilt for posterity.

Hand sew on the back of the quilt a sleeve for a rod if it is to be a wall hanging.

Now it's time to stand back and admire your handiwork, and impress your friends — just don't accept orders too quickly!

Care of your Quilt

When it comes time to wash the quilt, the family bath tub, minus the plastic duck, comes in very handy!

Dissolve wool mix or gentle detergent in warm water and soak your quilt for a short time, rinse and hang out on the line. Peg it well, inside out, or even use a trampoline to dry it flat in the shade.

If you're concerned about any fabrics running, then add a good quantity of salt (dissolved) to cold water and detergent, or colour fast check a scrap prior to washing.

Once the quilt has been completely dried and aired, do not fold but roll it, so you do not stress any seams. But as our quilts are in constant use, they don't have this problem!

Basic Embroidery Stitches

1.Cross Stitch

2.Lazy Daisy Stitch

3.Long Stitch

4.Stem Stitch

5.Bullion Roses

a)

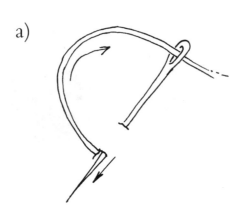

b)

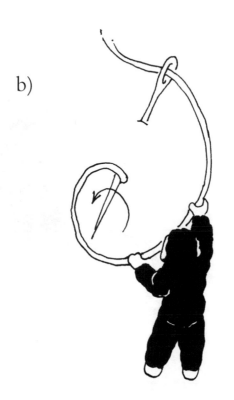

c)

d)

e)

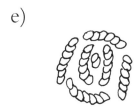

(See also French knot or Colonial knot on page 23. See also Blanket stitch, Back stitch and Running stitch on page 14.)

Acknowledgments

The majority of work was completed by ourselves, but without the kind help of the following people, our dreams and wishes for this book may not have come to fruition.

So to these people, we say thankyou:

Sewers and support team!

Helga Belser and Margaret Braddock (our mums), Therese McCallum, Karon Williams, Lyn McCallum, Marie Whittall, Cally McCallum and Di Barrie.

Photography

Clive Palmer, Jamestown SA

Frames

From recycled timber by Leanne and Bruce Walter Booleroo Centre SA. Can be contacted on (08) 8667 2239

Word Processing

Melissa McCallum

Proof-reading

Anne Nutt
Karen O'Dea
Michele Catford